THE BEARD BALLAD

HAROLD CRONK
ILLUSTRATIONS BY C.S. FRITZ

Beard Ballad
Copyright © 2018 by Harold Cronk

Published by Perfect Image
All rights reserved under the Pan-American and International Copyright Conventions. This book may not be reproduced in whole or in part, except for brief quotations embodied in critical articles or reviews, in any form or by any means, electronic or mechanical, including photocopying, recording, or by any information storage and retrieval system now known or hereinafter invented, without written permission of the author and the publisher.

Edited by Chip St.Clair
Story by Harold Cronk
Illustrations by C.S. Fritz

ISBN 978-0-578-58000-5
Printed in Canada through Bookmark

This book would never have happened
without the love and support of my amazing family.
Amy, Evy, and Harry...
thank you.

Foreword

I know what you're probably thinking. This book is all about manly things...like beards. And chopping wood in the great outdoors. And flannel. Lots of flannel.
Okay, maybe it is about those things. But more importantly it's about time. And the value of that time shared between father and son.

With this book, my Brother in Christ, Harold Cronk, has captured what it means to be a dad—to teach, to give, to share, and to love. Whether it's duck hunting, chopping wood, reading books, or growing beards together, that time spent between father and son is a gift. Maybe the most important gift a father can give his son. Because then you're growing more than beards. You're growing another man. And that kind of growing, that kind of investing in our sons' lives will pay huge dividends in the future for us all.

My boys and I have had some of our best times chopping wood and growing beards together. Hey, we still do. The older I get, the more I appreciate it. And they do, too.
Enjoy this book. My sons and grandsons sure did. It's more than just a bedtime story. It's a great reminder of the important role we play as fathers.
Happy growing!

- Phil Robertson

It was a blurry-eyed, blustery, frigid fall day,
and I could not have imagined what was headed my way.
My dad in his tie, all ready for work,
had entered the kitchen with a bit of a smirk.
It was then that I noticed his jaw and his chin
were covered in stubble, which he rubbed with a grin.

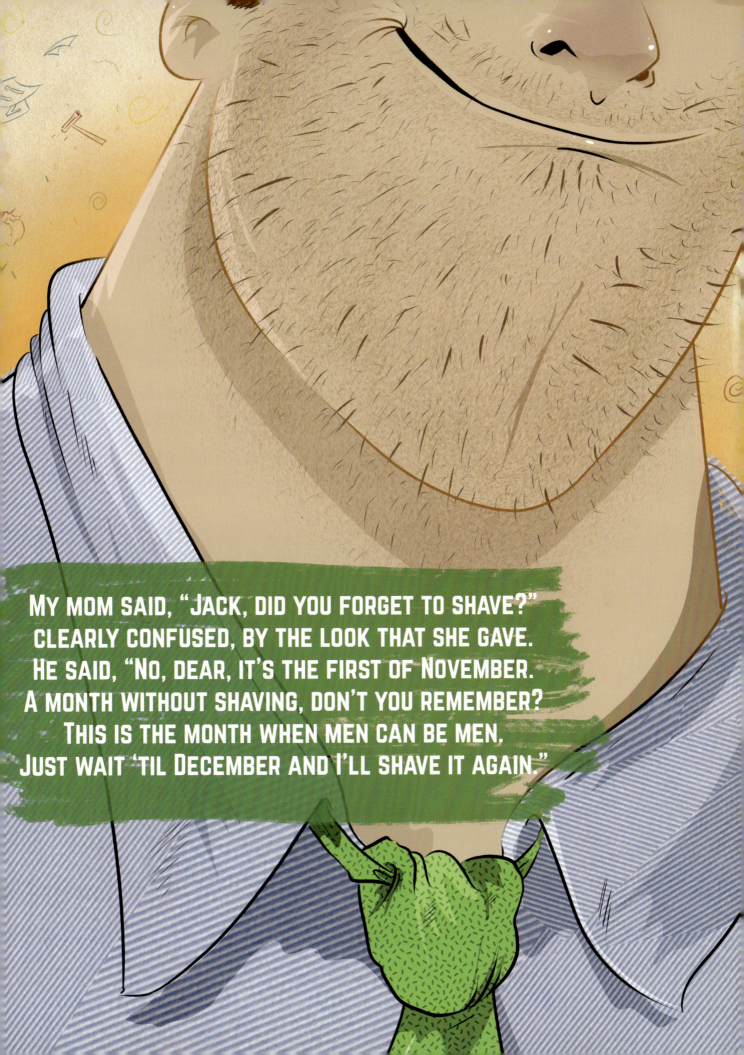

12 **The Big Bad Duck Daddy**
PHIL ROBERTSON APPROVED

11 **Santa Supreme**

10 **The Sweaty Yeti**

9 **Ferocious Facial Follicles**

8 **Grizzly Bear Chin Hair**

7 **Vile Viking Crumb Catcher**

6 **Mutton Chop Chin Crop**

5 **The Old Dutch Clutch**

4 **The Hairy Hipster**

3 **Mr. Whisker**

2 **Stubble Trouble**

1 **Peach Fuzz**

Mom's eyes grew huge
as she leapt from her chair.
"Oh, what will we do
with all of that hair?"
I said, "It's just a month, mom,
how bad could it be?"
She rolled her eyes,
then pointed to her knee.
"This is how long his beard
will soon be!"

And then I heard it, a melodic tune,
like happy young crickets, singing in June.
Those proud little hairs pushing up through the skin,
like pulling a bow across a concert violin.
I trembled and shouted as loud as I could,
"That beard song makes me want to chop wood!"

We chopped and we chopped as the days came and went.
In that woodpile we were making a dent!
I wiped my nose on my red checkered sleeve,
and what happened next you wouldn't believe!
That old flannel shirt stuck right to my face,
so I yanked it free to keep up the pace.

But then I realized why it had stuck.
I rubbed my cheek and I was in luck!
Short, strong hairs had started to grow!
They grabbed my sleeve and just wouldn't let go!
My first beard ballad, it had started to sing!
Faster and harder my axe I did swing!

We stacked and we stacked that pile of wood,
we stacked it just as high as we could!
Our dueling beard ballads drove us along.
A feeling this good just couldn't be wrong!
Sweat, muscles, smiles, and our shirts made of flannel
brought a joy not found on any TV channel.

For Dad,
who gave me more
than he could have ever imagined.

And to fathers everywhere:
your sacrifices, dedication, and love
are instrumental to the success
of future generations.

Thank you for all that you do.

Use your imagination to draw and color beards on the following pages.

What would your beard look like?

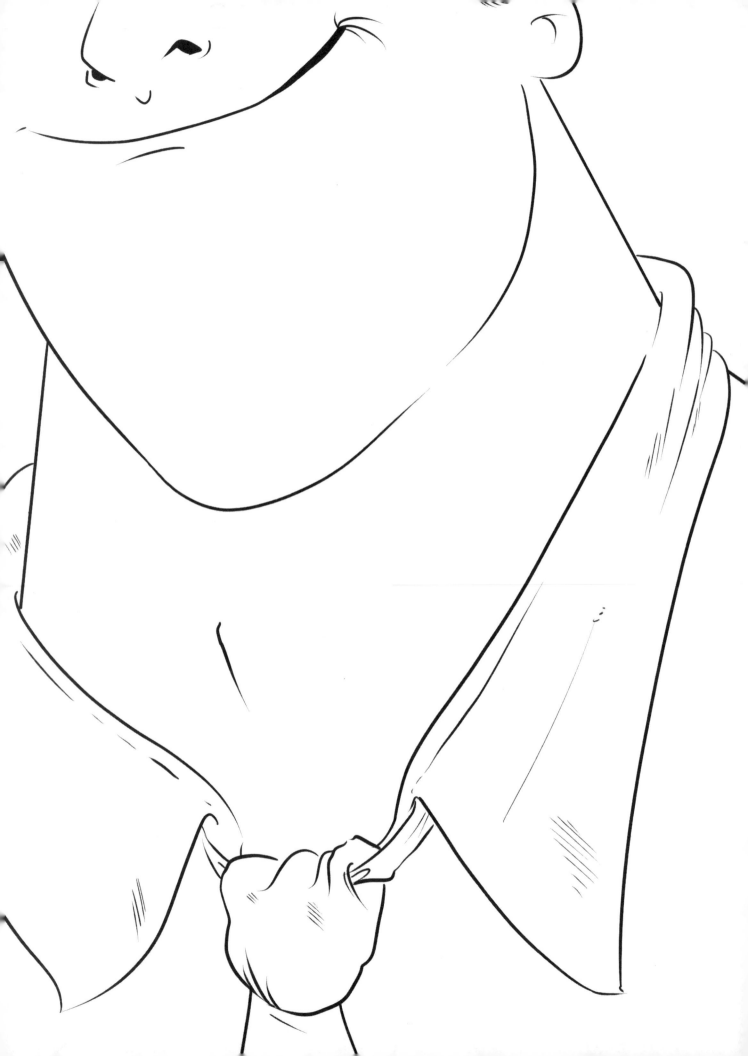

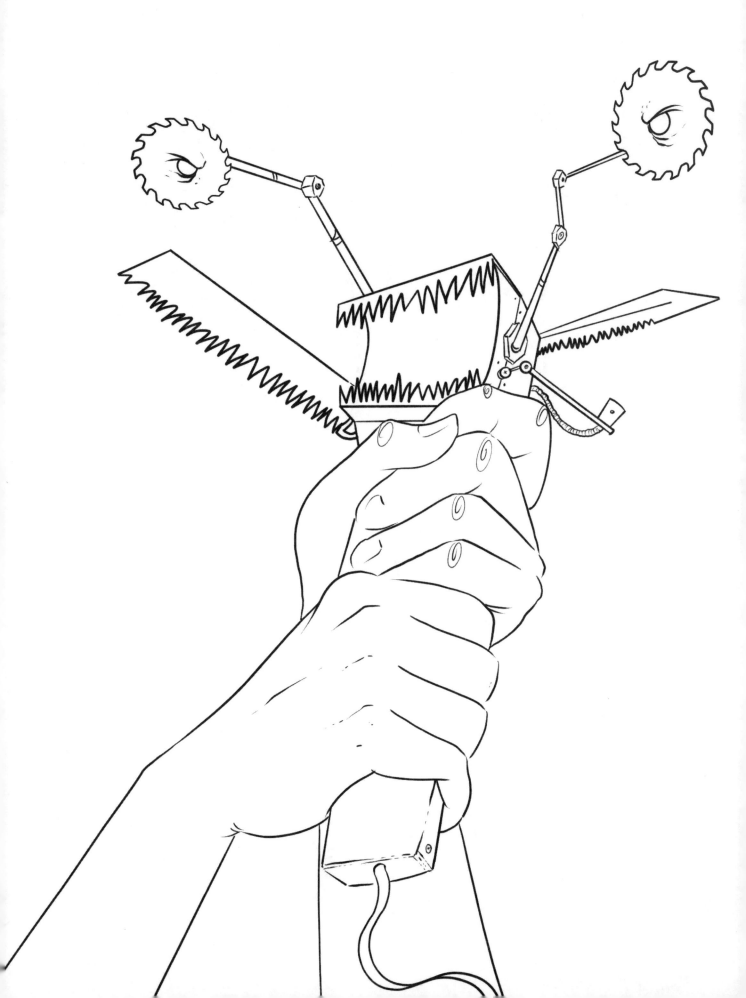